DAVID'S MIGHTY MEN

WARRIORS, COMPANIONS, AND LESSONS IN FAITH

CASPER WAMBOKO

David's Mighty Men

Casper Wamboko

Published by Delatech Solutions, 2023.

While every precaution has been taken in the preparation of this book, the publisher assumes no responsibility for errors or omissions, or for damages resulting from the use of the information contained herein.

DAVID'S MIGHTY MEN

First edition. July 18, 2023.

Copyright © 2023 Casper Wamboko.

ISBN: 979-8223751137

Written by Casper Wamboko.

Table of Contents

I would like to acknowledge God for giving me wisdom to write this book. I would also like to thank my family, for all the support I got from them, while I was writing this book.

David's Mighty Men

Chapter 1
David's Early Life

In the annals of history, few tales rival the valor and courage displayed by the mighty men of David. These legendary warriors, forged in the crucible of countless battles and united under the resplendent banner of their beloved king, have left an indelible mark on the pages of ancient scripture. Their tales echo through the corridors of time, resonating with the spirit of heroism and inspiring generations to come. Immortalized in the sacred Book of 2nd Samuel, Chapter 23, verse 8, their names and deeds are etched into the very fabric of Israel's storied past.

As we embark on this enlightening journey, we peel back the layers of time to uncover the remarkable lives of these individuals, who stood at the forefront of David's loyal entourage. These extraordinary men, whose unwavering loyalty knew no bounds, were more than mere soldiers. They were trusted confidants, esteemed advisors, and unyielding pillars of support for their esteemed leader. Their unbreakable bond with David exemplified the essence of camaraderie and unwavering dedication.

Amidst the tales of valor and triumph, we encounter a diverse tapestry of characters, each possessing unique strengths and skills. It is within this rich tapestry that we discover the intricacies of their relationships with David. We witness the sage wisdom imparted by the king, his nurturing guidance shaping the hearts and minds of these mighty warriors. David, himself a man after God's own heart, instilled within them the virtues of humility, faith, and unwavering trust in the divine providence that guided their every step.

Within the folds of this historical tapestry, we encounter not only the familiar names but also new revelations. Men like Abishai, renowned for his fierce loyalty and unwavering courage in battle, rise to prominence. His unwavering commitment to David's cause and his unyielding determination to protect his king became the stuff of legends. We also meet Joab, David's nephew, whose strategic brilliance and unshakable resolve proved instrumental in securing countless victories on the battlefield. These new characters serve to enrich the tapestry, adding depth and complexity to an already captivating narrative.

As we delve deeper into the lives of these remarkable individuals, we unearth the invaluable lessons they learned from their esteemed leader. From David, they imbibed the essence of integrity, honor, and righteousness. Their lives bore witness to the transformative power of humility, the unwavering strength found in unity, and the unbreakable bond forged in the crucible of adversity. Through their experiences, we glean timeless wisdom that transcends the boundaries of time and culture, reminding us of the enduring power of virtue and the indomitable spirit of the human soul.

In the following chapters, we will embark on a journey through the annals of history, traversing the battlegrounds, and delving into the hearts and minds of these legendary warriors. Their stories will inspire, captivate, and challenge us to embrace the virtues they so nobly embodied. So join us now, as we unveil the epic saga of the mighty men of David, a saga that continues to echo through the ages, reminding us that within the human spirit lies the potential for greatness and the capacity to leave an indelible mark on the world.

In this captivating chapter, we embark on a profound journey into the early life of David, a young shepherd who would ultimately be anointed by God as the future king of Israel. It is within these formative years that the foundation of David's character is laid, setting the stage for the extraordinary destiny that awaits him.

As we traverse the hills and valleys of Bethlehem, the birthplace of David, we witness a humble young man tending to his flock with unwavering devotion. It is in the solitude of the wilderness that David's intimate relationship with God begins to take root. The vibrant tapestry of nature becomes his sanctuary, where he finds solace and communion with the divine. The stars in the night sky bear witness to his whispered prayers, as he seeks guidance and strength for the journey ahead.

In the midst of his solitary existence, David's inherent leadership qualities begin to emerge. He navigates the treacherous terrain, protecting his flock from predators with unwavering courage and resourcefulness. His keen senses, honed by years of vigilant guardianship, enable him to anticipate danger and take swift, decisive action. These early experiences shape the seeds of leadership that are sown within him, preparing him for the weighty responsibilities that lie ahead.

While David's path may have initially seemed isolated, the threads of destiny begin to weave together when he encounters the remarkable individuals who would become his mighty men. These extraordinary warriors, with their own stories of triumph and hardship, are drawn to David's magnetic presence. Their spirits resonate with the youthful shepherd's unwavering faith and unwavering determination.

It is in their shared experiences that the bond between David and his mighty men begins to flourish. Their camaraderie deepens as they face trials and tribulations together, forging an unbreakable brotherhood. Each individual brings unique strengths and perspectives to the table, creating a synergy that propels them forward in their shared pursuit of justice and righteousness. The loyalty and trust that develop between them lay the foundation for a partnership that will withstand the tests of time.

As we immerse ourselves in the early chapters of David's extraordinary journey, we encounter not only the familiar figures but also new revelations. Characters like Jonathan, the valiant son of King Saul, step into the narrative, their lives intertwining with David's in unexpected ways. Their friendships bring new dimensions to the story, adding depth and complexity to the tapestry of David's life.

As the story continues, we will witness the trials and triumphs that shape David's character, his unwavering faith, and his unwavering commitment to God's purpose. We will walk alongside him as he faces daunting challenges, experiences profound loss, and emerges as a leader who will forever be etched in the annals of history. So join us now, as we embark on this transformative journey through the early life of David, where the seeds of destiny are sown, and the bonds of brotherhood are forged in the crucible of adversity.

Chapter 2
David's Mighty Men

In this captivating chapter, we embark on a profound exploration of the unique qualities that set apart the mighty men of David. These legendary warriors, whose names resonate through the annals of history, possess a remarkable blend of physical prowess, indomitable spirit, and unwavering devotion to their beloved king. Their exceptional abilities and unwavering loyalty make them a formidable force to be reckoned with.

Drawing from historical accounts and biblical narratives, we delve deep into the lives of these extraordinary individuals, seeking to uncover the secrets of their formidable skills. It is within the training grounds and battlefields that their true mettle is forged. These mighty men, chosen by David himself, undergo rigorous training and discipline, honing their bodies and minds for the challenges that await them.

Their physical prowess is unparalleled, their bodies honed through relentless training and rigorous conditioning. Endless hours are spent perfecting their skills with various weapons, mastering the art of swordplay, archery, and hand-to-hand combat. Their sinewy muscles ripple with power and their reflexes are lightning-fast, allowing them to strike with precision and accuracy in the heat of battle.

Yet, it is not merely their physical abilities that set them apart; it is their indomitable spirit that truly defines them. These warriors possess an unwavering determination and unyielding resolve, forged in the crucible of countless battles. They face adversity head-on, undeterred by fear or doubt, knowing that their cause is just and their king is worthy of their sacrifice. Their unwavering devotion to David fuels their spirits, propelling them to unimaginable feats of bravery and heroism.

Within the chapters of their lives, we encounter new revelations and individuals who add depth and complexity to their stories. Figures such as Joab, the fierce and strategic commander of David's army, emerges as a central figure in their exploits. His guidance and mentorship shape the tactics and battle strategies employed by these mighty men, amplifying their effectiveness on the battlefield.

Through vivid accounts and eye-witness testimonies, we witness the mighty men in action, as they face insurmountable odds with unwavering courage. They engage in epic battles, their swords flashing in the sun, arrows soaring through the air with deadly accuracy. Their unity and coordinated efforts transform them into an unstoppable force, striking fear into the hearts of their enemies.

As we journey through the rich tapestry of their lives, we come to understand that the might of these warriors is not solely derived from their physical prowess. It is their unwavering faith in their cause, their unyielding loyalty to their king, and their unwavering determination to uphold justice and righteousness that make them truly mighty. They embody the virtues of courage, honor, and selflessness, inspiring generations to come.

Join us now, as we unveil the remarkable qualities and astounding achievements of the mighty men of David. Through their stories, we discover the power of unwavering devotion, the triumph of indomitable spirit, and the enduring legacy of loyalty and valor. Prepare to be captivated by the extraordinary lives of these legendary warriors, whose names echo through the corridors of time.

In the vast tapestry of the mighty men's tales, one figure stands out as a force to be reckoned with: Joab, a warrior of immense skill and complexity. Within the folds of this chapter, we dedicate our attention to unraveling the enigma that is Joab. As a central figure among the mighty men, his story warrants its own exploration, for it is within his life that we find a captivating blend of loyalty, cunning, and the burden of consequence.

At the heart of Joab's narrative lies his intricate relationship with David, the beloved king of Israel. We delve into the depths of their connection, navigating the ebbs and flows of trust, friendship, and rivalry that shaped their dynamic. Joab's loyalty to David was unwavering, bound by the ties of brotherhood forged through countless battles. Yet, it is within the complexities of their bond that we unearth a profound exploration of the intricacies of loyalty itself.

As the commander of the Israelite army, Joab was entrusted with the responsibility of leading the mighty men into battle. His strategic acumen, combined with his unparalleled ferocity on the battlefield, earned him a reputation that echoed throughout the land. In the midst of the chaos and bloodshed, Joab emerged as a figure of fear and respect, his cunning and tactical brilliance instrumental in securing numerous victories for the kingdom.

However, it is through Joab's interactions with David that we witness the intertwining threads of their lives. The lessons he gleaned from his revered king were both profound and bittersweet. David's wisdom, acquired through his own trials and tribulations, served as a beacon of guidance for Joab. He learned the art of leadership, the delicate balance between justice and mercy, and the weight of decisions that can shape the course of nations.

Yet, as with any tale of heroes, shadows loom on the periphery. Joab's story is not without its share of consequences and moral dilemmas. His unwavering loyalty, at times, led him down a path that bore the burden of questionable actions. In the face of adversity, Joab made choices that would reverberate through the annals of history, leaving a lasting mark on his legacy.

Within this chapter, we navigate the complexities of Joab's character, exploring the shades of gray that define his journey. His fierce determination and strategic brilliance were tempered by the consequences of his choices, reminding us of the intricate dance between loyalty and accountability. Through his experiences, we are challenged to reflect upon the complexities of leadership, the moral quandaries that arise in times of conflict, and the lasting impact of our actions.

Join us now as we embark on an immersive exploration of Joab's life, where loyalty and leadership collide, and the lessons learned from David's tutelage are put to the ultimate test. Delve into the intricacies of this enigmatic figure, as we unravel the multifaceted layers that make up the tale of Joab, the mighty warrior and complex soul whose story reverberates through the corridors of history.

We embark on an exhilarating journey into the legendary ranks of the "Three and Thirty," an elite group of warriors whose names have become synonymous with heroism and valor. As we peel back the layers of history, we uncover the extraordinary lives and remarkable achievements of individuals who etched their names in the annals of glory. Among these distinguished figures are Josheb-Basshebeth, Eleazar, and Shammah, whose tales are woven with threads of courage, sacrifice, and unwavering determination.

Josheb-Basshebeth, a name that resonates with power and prowess, stands as a shining example of the indomitable spirit that defined the mighty men of David. With a blade as swift as lightning and a heart that knew no fear, he carved a path of victory on the battlefield. His unwavering loyalty to David was matched only by his unwavering faith in the cause they fought for. Through his unparalleled feats of strength and strategic brilliance, Josheb-Basshebeth left an indelible mark on the sands of time.

Alongside Josheb-Basshebeth, we encounter the towering figure of Eleazar, a warrior whose courage knew no bounds. In the heat of battle, his sword was a force of divine justice, striking down the enemies of Israel with unwavering precision. Eleazar's unwavering commitment to righteousness and his unyielding resolve made him a beacon of inspiration for his fellow warriors. His unwavering dedication to the cause of justice served as a guiding light, illuminating the path to victory even in the darkest of times.

And then there was Shammah, a steadfast warrior whose name echoed through the ranks of the mighty men. His unwavering determination and unbreakable spirit were the hallmarks of his character. With his back against the wall and his comrades by his side, Shammah stood resolute, defending the very ground that symbolized their unity. His unwavering loyalty to his fellow warriors and his unyielding commitment to the cause of David made him a formidable force on the battlefield.

DAVID'S MIGHTY MEN

Within the folds of this chapter, we bear witness to the awe-inspiring exploits of these extraordinary individuals and their fellow warriors. Their stories are not merely tales of bravery and heroism, but windows into the human spirit, showcasing the heights that can be reached when courage and conviction merge as one. Through the pages of historical accounts and biblical narratives, we are transported to a time when the clash of steel and the roar of battle resonated in the hearts of these mighty men.

Together, the "Three and Thirty" formed an indomitable brotherhood, bonded by a shared purpose and a common destiny. They exemplified the virtues of honor, loyalty, and unwavering resolve, leaving an enduring legacy that continues to inspire generations to this day. Their exploits on the battlefield, fueled by an indomitable spirit, serve as a reminder that greatness can be achieved through unwavering dedication and the pursuit of a noble cause.

Join us now as we delve into the lives and achievements of these extraordinary warriors, traversing the realms of history and faith to uncover the stories of Josheb-Basshebeth, Eleazar, Shammah, and the countless others who comprised the ranks of the "Three and Thirty." Through their awe-inspiring exploits and unwavering valor, we shall bear witness to the indomitable human spirit and the extraordinary heights it can reach when fueled by unwavering courage and unwavering devotion.

In the vast tapestry of David's reign, his impact on the mighty men transcended the realm of warfare. This chapter serves as a gateway into the depths of wisdom, character, and faith that David imparted to his loyal companions. Beyond their physical prowess, it was the intangible qualities that set them apart as extraordinary individuals. With reverence, we embark on a journey that uncovers the profound influence of David's teachings and the transformative power they held.

Integrity, like a glistening beacon, illuminated the path that David walked. As the mighty men observed their beloved king, they witnessed a man whose actions aligned with his words, a man of unyielding moral fiber. Through countless encounters with adversity, David never wavered in his commitment to truth and righteousness. His unwavering adherence to principles became the cornerstone upon which the mighty men built their own lives.

Alongside integrity, humility found its rightful place in David's repertoire of virtues. Though an anointed king, he remained grounded, never succumbing to the allure of power and prestige. In the presence of his mighty men, David exemplified the essence of humility, treating each individual with respect and dignity. His willingness to listen, learn, and acknowledge the strengths of others fostered an environment of camaraderie and mutual growth.

Above all, it was David's unwavering trust in God that fueled his unwavering resolve. From the depths of the shepherd's fields to the heights of the throne, he clung to his faith, seeking solace and guidance in the divine. It was through David's unwavering trust in God that the mighty men learned the significance of surrendering their fears and doubts, placing their destinies in the hands of a higher power. In the crucible of trials, their faith was tested, and through David's example, they discovered the wellspring of strength that lay within their hearts.

Within the sacred bonds between David and his mighty men, lessons were exchanged and learned. The mighty men, in turn, absorbed the wisdom of their king, melding it with their own experiences and insights. As the chapters of their lives unfolded, they carried the torch of David's teachings, spreading his wisdom like wildfire among their fellow warriors. The impact of David's influence reached far and wide, extending beyond the confines of the battlefield to touch the lives of countless souls.

In the midst of our exploration, we encounter new faces and revelations, individuals whose lives were intertwined with the mighty men and whose stories have been interwoven with the legacy of David. These figures, whether commanders, strategists, or advisors, added depth and richness to the collective narrative of the mighty men. Their unique perspectives and contributions serve as reminders of the diverse tapestry of personalities that comprised David's inner circle.

Join us now as we venture into the heart of this chapter, navigating the intertwining threads of wisdom, character, and faith that defined David's relationship with his mighty men. Through the lens of their experiences, we shall witness the transformative power of integrity, humility, and unwavering trust in God. In their stories, we shall find echoes of our own journeys, drawing inspiration from the timeless teachings that continue to resonate through the corridors of history. We find ourselves immersed in the profound reflection of the lasting legacy left behind by the mighty men of David. Beyond their extraordinary feats of valor, their impact resonated far and wide, shaping the very fabric of the nation of Israel. This chapter serves as a testament to their unwavering commitment, as we delve into their continued service under subsequent kings, their indomitable spirit driving them forward in their noble pursuits.

The stories of the mighty men continued to unfold even after the reign of David, their revered names whispered in awe and admiration. With each passing generation, their heroic deeds became the stuff of legends, inspiring new waves of warriors who sought to emulate their courage and dedication. Under the leadership of subsequent kings, these mighty men stood as beacons of strength, their experiences and wisdom sought after by those in positions of power.

Amidst the ebb and flow of political landscapes, the mighty men remained steadfast, offering their expertise and unwavering loyalty to the rulers who followed in David's footsteps. Their unparalleled skill on the battlefield, coupled with their unwavering sense of duty, ensured that their contributions continued to shape the destiny of the nation they so fiercely protected. Kings sought their counsel, armies rallied behind their banners, and enemies trembled at the mere mention of their names.

But it was not just their martial prowess that etched their names into the annals of history. The spiritual and moral lessons gleaned from the lives of these extraordinary individuals continue to reverberate through the ages. Their unwavering faith in God, their commitment to justice, and their embodiment of honorable virtues serve as guiding lights in the darkness of our own lives. In their stories, we find solace and inspiration, reminding us of the potential that lies within each of us to rise above adversity and make a lasting impact.

It is within these tales of heroism that we encounter new revelations, individuals whose lives intertwined with those of the mighty men, leaving an indelible mark on their journeys. We are introduced to warriors who followed in their footsteps, disciples who learned from their teachings, and leaders who carried forward their legacy. Their unique perspectives and contributions add depth to the tapestry of the mighty men's saga, underscoring the interconnectedness of their lives and the wider impact of their actions.

As we bring this chapter to a close, we find ourselves contemplating the timeless relevance of the mighty men's stories. Their lives continue to inspire and challenge us, urging us to embrace courage, honor, and unwavering loyalty in the face of adversity. The legacy they left behind serves as a reminder of the transformative power of individuals who choose to stand for what is right, regardless of the circumstances. May their stories continue to echo through the corridors of time, igniting the flames of bravery and righteousness in the hearts of generations to come.

The mighty men of David were more than mere soldiers; they were exemplars of valor, loyalty, and faith. Their stories serve as a timeless reminder of the power of conviction, the strength of brotherhood, and the enduring legacy of those who walk in faith. Through their exploits and the lessons they learned from David, we gain insights into what it truly means to live a life of courage, purpose, and unwavering devotion. The tales of the mighty men of David will forever stand as a testament to the triumph of the human spirit and the eternal power of faith.

The mighty men of David were not just ordinary soldiers; they embodied the very essence of valor, loyalty

DAVID'S MIGHTY MEN

The mighty men of David, revered throughout the ages, transcended the realm of ordinary soldiers. Their indomitable spirit and unwavering commitment to their cause elevated them to the status of exemplars - embodiments of valor, loyalty, and faith. Their stories, handed down through generations, have become a cherished part of our collective heritage, serving as a timeless reminder of the extraordinary potential that lies within each of us.

In the annals of history, their names are etched in golden letters, forever memorializing their remarkable feats of bravery and sacrifice. From Eleazar, whose hand clung to his sword amidst a battlefield, to Shammah, who defended a plot of lentils single-handedly, their acts of courage defy human comprehension. These mighty men stood as beacons of inspiration, demonstrating that true heroism arises not from the absence of fear, but from the unwavering resolve to confront it head-on.

Beyond their physical prowess, it was their unyielding faith that set them apart. Rooted in the teachings and guidance of their beloved king, David, they drew strength from a higher power, recognizing that their victories were not solely the result of their own might, but a manifestation of the divine working through them. Through their unwavering devotion, they became vessels through which the power of faith flowed, lighting a path for others to follow.

The camaraderie shared among the mighty men was an integral part of their journey. Their brotherhood extended beyond the battlefield, forged through shared experiences and a common purpose. Each member of this esteemed group understood the significance of unity and the power of standing shoulder to shoulder with those who shared their ideals. Together, they formed an unbreakable bond, each one contributing their unique strengths to the collective whole.

In the crucible of their interactions with David, these mighty men imbibed invaluable lessons that transcended the realm of warfare. They witnessed firsthand David's unwavering commitment to integrity, his humility in the face of adversity, and his unshakeable trust in the Almighty. From their beloved king, they learned that true strength arises not from physical might alone, but from a heart aligned with righteousness and a spirit attuned to the divine.

The tales of the mighty men of David, passed down through generations, continue to captivate and inspire. Their stories resonate with us, for they touch upon timeless truths and universal principles that transcend the boundaries of time and culture. They remind us that courage, purpose, and unwavering devotion are not relics of a bygone era but virtues that are as relevant today as they were centuries ago.

As we reflect upon the legacy of these mighty men, we are beckoned to introspection. Their lives challenge us to examine our own convictions, to cultivate a spirit of unwavering loyalty, and to embrace the power of faith. They call us to rise above mediocrity, to confront the challenges that lie before us with resolute determination, and to leave an enduring mark upon the tapestry of human history.

The tales of the mighty men of David, with their triumphs and struggles, their unwavering faith and unwavering devotion, serve as a testament to the indomitable nature of the human spirit and the eternal power of faith. They remind us that within each of us lies the potential for greatness, waiting to be awakened by a purpose greater than ourselves. May their stories continue to inspire, guide, and ignite the flame of courage within us all.

In the vast tapestry of history, few narratives resound with the resolute valor and indomitable heroism exhibited by the Three Mighty Men of David. These revered and legendary warriors, carefully handpicked from the ranks of David's unwavering devotees, have etched their names in the hallowed annals of Israel's storied past. From the depths of their souls, they conjured feats of unparalleled bravery and valor that have reverberated through the ages. The sacred verses of the Book of 2nd Samuel, Chapter 23, verse 8, stand as an enduring testament to their unwavering loyalty and their profound impact upon the kingdom of Israel.

As the pages of this book unfurl, we embark on a transformative journey, a pilgrimage through time that shall unveil the extraordinary lives of these exceptional individuals. With each turn of the page, we traverse their footsteps, delving into the triumphs and tribulations that forged their indelible legacies. Like the strands of a tapestry woven with divine threads, their lives interweave with the fate of a nation, illuminating the path of righteousness, sacrifice, and unwavering devotion.

Among the Three Mighty Men, we encounter Josheb-Basshebeth, an invincible warrior whose spear struck terror into the hearts of their adversaries. His mere presence on the battlefield instilled a fierce determination in his comrades, for they knew that alongside him, victory was within reach. Eleazar, whose unwavering commitment to the cause of his beloved king and nation surpassed all bounds, stood as an immovable pillar of strength. His valor knew no bounds, even in the face of overwhelming odds. And Shammah, the embodiment of steadfastness, fiercely defended a plot of lentils against a horde of enemy warriors. His unyielding resolve and unwavering loyalty made him a symbol of inspiration to all who bore witness.

The bond shared between these mighty men and David transcended that of mere soldiers and their king. It was an unbreakable covenant forged in the crucible of shared trials and victories. Their lives intertwined in a symphony of loyalty, trust, and mutual respect, a bond fortified by the trials they faced together. David, a shepherd who ascended to the throne of Israel, served not only as their leader but as a beacon of wisdom, guidance, and inspiration. Through his exemplary character, he nurtured within them the virtues of honor, humility, and unshakable faith, molding them into the warriors they would become.

Within the pages of this book, we shall witness their extraordinary feats, their moments of triumph that reverberated through the annals of time. But it is not merely their physical prowess that shall captivate us; it is the invaluable lessons they imbibed from their esteemed leader that truly make them legendary. From David, they learned the importance of integrity, righteousness, and the unyielding pursuit of justice. Their lives became a testament to the enduring power of these virtues, a beacon to guide subsequent generations in their quest for righteousness.

As we embark on this transformative journey, we bear witness to the intertwining tapestry of history, faith, and valor. The Three Mighty Men of David, with their unwavering loyalty, unparalleled bravery, and unyielding devotion, continue to inspire and challenge us in our own paths. Their stories are not merely accounts of distant heroes but a living testament to the potential that lies dormant within each of us. May their indomitable spirit guide us on our own quests for courage, honor, and unwavering devotion.

This chapter delves into the intricacies of the upbringing and formative experiences of the illustrious Three Mighty Men. Like brushstrokes on a canvas, we paint a vivid and intricate picture of their diverse backgrounds, each possessing a unique tapestry of life's trials and triumphs. From the rolling hills of Josheb-Basshebeth's homeland to the bustling streets of Eleazar's city, and the serene countryside of Shammah's village, we uncover the threads that wove their lives together in the grand tapestry of destiny.

Josheb-Basshebeth, hailing from a lineage of valiant warriors, grew up in a household that celebrated strength, valor, and the pursuit of justice. His father regaled him with tales of battles fought and victories won, instilling within him a sense of honor and a burning desire to leave his mark on the pages of history. As he stood atop the hills, gazing out at the vast expanse of his homeland, the young Josheb-Basshebeth felt the weight of responsibility settle upon his shoulders, knowing that he was destined for greatness.

In a bustling city teeming with ambition, Eleazar was born into a family of artisans. His father, a skilled blacksmith, imparted to him the virtues of craftsmanship, discipline, and dedication. As a child, Eleazar spent countless hours in his father's workshop, honing his skills and channeling his passion into creating works of art. Little did he know that these lessons in patience, precision, and unwavering focus would serve him well in the days to come when he would wield his weapons with the same artistry as a master craftsman.

Shammah, on the other hand, grew up in the simplicity of a humble village, surrounded by vast fields and gentle streams. His days were filled with tending to the family's flock, wandering the verdant meadows, and seeking solace in the quietude of nature. It was in these serene surroundings that Shammah cultivated a deep connection with the land, fostering within him a profound understanding of perseverance and the beauty that lies within the seemingly ordinary. Little did he know that these tranquil moments would become the foundation of his unyielding spirit on the battlefield.

As we peel back the layers of time, we witness the fortuitous encounters that led these extraordinary individuals to the side of David, the future king. A chance meeting on a bustling marketplace, a fateful encounter on the outskirts of a village, and a shared moment of destiny in the heat of battle—each path converging to a singular moment that would forever alter their lives. United under David's banner, they found purpose, camaraderie, and a sense of belonging that had eluded them until that very moment.

It is in the crucible of their upbringing, the diverse tapestry of their experiences, and the nurturing guidance of David that the qualities distinguishing these men were forged. While still in the bloom of youth, they exhibited extraordinary strength of character, unwavering loyalty, and an unquenchable thirst for righteousness. From the wisdom of their elders to the trials they faced on their individual journeys, each step prepared them for the destiny that awaited them, molding them into the legendary warriors they would become.

Through the wisdom of historical accounts and ancient writings, we piece together the fragments of their past, illuminating the winding paths that led them to David's side. It is within these chapters that we uncover the roots of their noble spirits and the unique qualities that set them apart, even before they were called upon to wield their swords and shields. As we embark on this journey of discovery, we come to understand that their journey was not one of happenstance, but a carefully orchestrated tapestry woven by the hands of destiny itself.

Chapter 3
The Three Mighty Men Of David

At the very heart of the extraordinary relationship that bound the Three Mighty Men to David, a covenant of unwavering loyalty was forged, surpassing the bounds of mere comradeship. As we delve into this chapter, the tapestry of their connection unfurls, revealing the profound depths of their bond. Through the annals of time, we journey alongside these warriors, witnessing the shared experiences that etched indelible marks upon their souls and forever intertwined their destinies.

Amidst the chaos of battle, when the clash of swords resounded and the air was thick with the scent of sweat and iron, they stood shoulder to shoulder, a formidable force united by a common purpose. It was in these moments, amidst the tumultuous storm of warfare, that the seeds of their unyielding commitment were sown. Together, they weathered the onslaught of adversaries, their lives intertwining in a dance of strength, courage, and unwavering determination.

As we venture further into their narrative, we encounter a revelation—an addition to their illustrious ranks. In the midst of a heated conflict, a valiant warrior emerged from the shadows, his name whispered in hushed tones among the men. It was Azariah, a man of exceptional skill and unyielding resolve. His arrival breathed new life into the brotherhood, infusing their ranks with an invigorating spirit. With each battle fought side by side, Azariah's loyalty to David and his mighty companions became a pillar of their collective strength.

Anecdote after anecdote reveals the extraordinary lengths to which these warriors went to protect and honor their king. Whether it was Eleazar, single-handedly defending a barley field against overwhelming odds or Shammah, standing his ground in the face of an onslaught to protect a patch of lentils, their commitment to safeguarding what was entrusted to them was unwavering. Through these tales, we witness the undeniable bond that shaped their interactions, their sacrifices, and their unspoken understanding of one another.

David, in turn, recognized the immeasurable worth of these loyal warriors. His leadership and guidance became a beacon, guiding their steps through the darkness of uncertainty. It was through David's unwavering belief in their abilities, his unwavering trust in their loyalty, that the Three Mighty Men found the strength to conquer insurmountable odds. David's wisdom, forged in the crucible of his own experiences, became a wellspring from which they drew inspiration, enabling them to rise above the chaos of battle and embrace their destiny as legendary warriors.

Through the ancient records and historical accounts that have withstood the test of time, we bear witness to the loyalty and devotion that wove these men together into a brotherhood bound by an unbreakable covenant. Their shared experiences, the triumphs and tragedies they faced side by side, became the very threads that stitched their hearts together. It was this unshakeable bond, fortified by their mutual respect and unwavering commitment, that propelled them to extraordinary heights, transforming them into an immortal symbol of loyalty and brotherhood.

As we turn the pages of this chapter, we are reminded that true loyalty knows no bounds. It surpasses the confines of time, transcends the boundaries of circumstance, and echoes through the ages as a testament to the enduring power of devotion. In the tales of the Three Mighty Men, we find not only a testament to their unparalleled valor but a profound exploration of the human spirit and the extraordinary heights it can reach when fueled by the bonds of unwavering loyalty.

This chapter delves deep into the extraordinary life of Adino, the first among the Three Mighty Men. As we embark on this journey of discovery, we unveil the multifaceted layers that defined this legendary warrior. Known far and wide for his unmatched bravery and unyielding courage, Adino's presence on the battlefield was nothing short of awe-inspiring.

Amidst the chaos of war, when the clash of weapons reverberated through the air and the ground shook with the weight of impending doom, Adino stood as a beacon of unwavering resolve. It was in these harrowing moments that his indomitable spirit shone brightly, driving fear into the hearts of his enemies and igniting hope in the souls of his comrades.

In the ancient annals of Israel, amidst the accounts of mighty warriors and their awe-inspiring feats, there is a tale of one man whose valor and skill stood out among them all. His name was Adino, the Eznite, and his story is etched in the sacred scriptures in 2nd Samuel 23, verse 8.

Adino, a man of extraordinary strength and unwavering determination, was destined to leave an indelible mark on the battlefield. On that fateful day, as the sun rose over the horizon, a formidable enemy force loomed before the ranks of Israel. The air was thick with tension and the ground trembled with anticipation. It was a moment that would test the mettle of warriors and define their place in history.

Armed with his trusty spear, Adino stood tall and resolute amidst the chaos of battle. With unwavering focus, he surveyed the scene before him, his eyes alight with a fire that burned within his soul. The enemy ranks advanced, a wave of fierce adversaries intent on overpowering the Israelite forces.

But Adino, undeterred by the overwhelming odds, summoned his inner strength and unleashed a fury that seemed supernatural. With each swing of his spear, he struck down his foes with precision and unmatched skill. The battlefield became a canvas upon which his might was displayed, his every movement calculated and purposeful.

As the clash of weapons resounded in the air, Adino's spear became an extension of his very being, a conduit for his unwavering resolve. His strikes were swift and true, finding their mark with deadly accuracy. One after another, his adversaries fell, their ranks thinning with each passing moment.

In an awe-inspiring display of prowess, Adino's spear became a blur of motion, a dance of death and victory. Eight hundred enemies succumbed to his relentless assault, their lives extinguished by his unyielding determination. The magnitude of his accomplishment reverberated through the ranks of both friend and foe, leaving all in awe of his unparalleled valor.

As the dust settled and the echoes of battle faded, Adino stood amidst the fallen, a testament to his unwavering courage and indomitable spirit. His feat would forever be etched into the annals of history, a testament to the power of a single individual's determination and skill.

Adino, the Eznite, became a legend, a figure whose name would be whispered with reverence among warriors and storytellers alike. His remarkable achievement would inspire generations to come, reminding them of the extraordinary heights that can be reached when one dares to dream, believes in their abilities, and fights with unwavering resolve.

So, let the tale of Adino, the mighty warrior who single-handedly felled eight hundred foes with his spear, echo through the ages, an emblem of valor and triumph in the face of overwhelming odds. May his story continue to inspire and ignite the flames of courage within the hearts of all who hear it, reminding us that within each of us lies the potential for extraordinary deeds.

But behind every great warrior lies a mentor who shapes their path. In the midst of Adino's tumultuous journey, David, the renowned king and leader, emerged as a guiding light. Their bond was forged through shared experiences and mutual respect, and it was through David's wisdom that Adino honed his skills and refined his approach to warfare and leadership.

Throughout their time together, David imparted invaluable lessons to Adino, drawing from his own vast well of experiences. The young warrior absorbed these teachings with an insatiable thirst for knowledge, understanding that true strength lies not only in physical prowess but also in strategic thinking and unwavering loyalty. From David, Adino learned the art of discernment, the importance of calculated risks, and the significance of leading with honor and integrity.

In the annals of battle, Adino's exploits etched their place in history. From the chaos of the battlefield, tales of his daring charges and unwavering determination spread like wildfire, capturing the imagination of generations to come. Time and again, he faced overwhelming odds, yet his unyielding spirit propelled him forward, inspiring those around him to fight with renewed vigor. The stories of Adino's triumphs became legendary, serving as a testament to the extraordinary heights one can achieve through unwavering courage and unwavering loyalty.

But beyond the battlefield, Adino's legacy transcended the realm of warfare. His unwavering devotion to his fellow warriors and his unshakable commitment to the cause exemplified the essence of true leadership. Through his actions, he inspired others to rise above their limitations, to tap into their inner reservoirs of strength, and to embrace the indomitable spirit that resides within each of us.

As we delve deeper into the life and legacy of Adino, we discover the complex tapestry of his character—the interplay of strength and vulnerability, bravery and compassion. His journey serves as a timeless reminder that greatness is not solely defined by physical might, but by the unwavering spirit and the steadfast commitment to a cause greater than oneself. We bear witness to the remarkable transformation of

Adino, from a young warrior molded by David's teachings to a legendary figure whose name would be spoken with reverence for generations to come. Through his exploits, we gain insights into the indomitable human spirit, the power of mentorship, and the resolute determination that can shape the course of history.

Adino's legacy continues to inspire, serving as a beacon of hope and a reminder that even in the face of insurmountable odds, courage and unwavering loyalty can pave the way to victory. His story echoes through the corridors of time, forever etching his name alongside the great heroes of old, and reminding us that within each of us lies the potential to become a mighty warrior in our own right.

In the annals of courage and unwavering loyalty, the name Eleazar stands tall among the heroes of Israel. In this chapter, we immerse ourselves in the remarkable life of the second of the Three Mighty Men, whose exploits echoed through the ages. Eleazar's unwavering commitment to defending the honor of Israel forged a path of valor that would leave an indelible mark on history.

Amidst the turbulent backdrop of ancient battles, Eleazar's unwavering determination shone brightly. His legendary stand against the Philistines became the stuff of legends, as he fearlessly faced a multitude of foes, his sword gleaming in the sunlight as he fought with unmatched ferocity. It was in these defining moments that Eleazar's steadfast loyalty to David's cause was displayed, his actions speaking volumes about his unwavering faith and dedication.

In the sacred scriptures of 2nd Samuel 23, verses 9 and 10, a tale unfolds of a warrior whose valor and unwavering dedication to his people set him apart from the rest. His name was Eleazar, and his story is one of extraordinary bravery and unwavering commitment in the face of overwhelming odds.

It was a time when the land of Israel was plagued by the presence of the Philistines, formidable adversaries who sought to assert their dominance over the Israelite people. In the midst of the battle, when the men of Israel retreated, Eleazar remained steadfast, standing alone against the onslaught of the enemy.

With his hand tightly gripping his sword, Eleazar fought with a ferocity that seemed superhuman. His heart burned with an unyielding determination to protect his people and defend their land. As the Philistines closed in, their numbers seemed insurmountable, yet Eleazar refused to falter.

The clash of steel echoed through the air as Eleazar, his grip unwavering, unleashed a torrent of blows upon his enemies. With each swing of his sword, he felled one adversary after another, his skill and strength unmatched. The Philistines, taken aback by his resolute stance and unparalleled prowess, were forced to reckon with the indomitable spirit of this lone warrior.

But as the battle raged on, the weariness began to take its toll on Eleazar. His arm grew heavy, his muscles strained under the weight of his relentless strikes. Yet, despite the physical toll, his resolve remained unshaken. Eleazar's hand became one with his sword, as if the two were inseparable, a testament to his unwavering commitment to his people and their cause.

As the dust settled and the cries of battle subsided, the ground lay scattered with fallen Philistines, each a testament to the ferocity and unwavering determination of Eleazar. His unwavering courage and fortitude had turned the tides of battle, leaving the Philistines in disarray and their forces scattered.

When the men of Israel returned to the field of battle, they were awestruck by the scene that lay before them. Eleazar, bloodied and battered, stood alone amidst the fallen, his hand still firmly gripping his sword. They hailed him as a hero, a symbol of unwavering bravery and devotion to the cause of their people.

Eleazar's selfless act of valor and his refusal to abandon his post even in the face of certain peril would forever be remembered in the annals of Israel's history. His story would inspire generations to come, a shining example of the triumph of courage and loyalty over adversity.

So, let the tale of Eleazar, the warrior whose hand clung to his sword while the men of Israel had left him alone, echo through the ages as a testament to the power of unwavering dedication and unyielding bravery. May his story inspire us all to stand firm in the face of adversity and fight for what we believe in, knowing that even in the darkest of times, true heroes can emerge.

But it was not only in the grand battles that Eleazar's courage was showcased; it was also in the seemingly ordinary moments that his true character revealed itself. One such moment was his resolute defense of a humble barley field. While others may have deemed it insignificant, Eleazar saw the value in protecting every inch of his beloved land. With unyielding resolve, he stood his ground, his unwavering determination inspiring those around him to fight with renewed vigor.

Behind every hero lies a mentor who shapes their destiny, and for Eleazar, that mentor was David. From the renowned king, Eleazar imbibed invaluable lessons that would forever shape his character and fortify his resolve. Through David's wisdom, he learned the importance of honor, loyalty, and the unwavering faith that anchors one's soul even in the face of adversity. It was these teachings that ignited a fire within Eleazar's heart, driving him to greatness on and off the battlefield.

As we journey deeper into Eleazar's story, we uncover the layers of his character, the complexities that make him more than just a fearless warrior. Beneath the surface of his valor, we find a man of compassion and empathy, whose heart beat with a profound love for his people and his land. He saw his duty not merely as a defender of physical boundaries, but also as a protector of the values and ideals that defined Israel.

Eleazar's legacy lives on, resonating through the ages as a testament to the power of unwavering loyalty and unshakable faith. His remarkable acts of valor continue to inspire generations, reminding us of the heights that can be reached when we dedicate ourselves to a noble cause.

Through his story, we gain insights into the indomitable human spirit, the resilience of the human heart, and the transformative power of unwavering commitment.

In this chapter, we bear witness to the extraordinary journey of Eleazar, a man whose unwavering commitment to his people and his cause set him apart as a true hero. His acts of valor and the lessons he learned from David serve as a timeless reminder that greatness is not bestowed upon a select few, but is within the reach of all those who dare to embrace their inner strength and stand for what they believe in.

As we explore Eleazar's life and legacy, we are captivated by the intricate tapestry of his character and the profound impact he had on the kingdom of Israel. His unwavering determination, his unyielding loyalty, and his unshakable faith continue to inspire and challenge us to this day. Eleazar's story is a testament to the enduring power of the human spirit, a beacon of hope that reminds us that even in the face of insurmountable odds, we too can rise as mighty warriors in our own lives.

In the realm of the Three Mighty Men, a figure of remarkable steadfastness and resilience emerges—Shammah. While often overlooked, his story is a testament to unwavering dedication and the power of unwavering commitment. In this chapter, we delve into the extraordinary life of Shammah, uncovering the depths of his character and the indomitable spirit that defined him.

Shammah's defining moment came during a harrowing battle against the relentless Philistine army. It was in defense of a seemingly insignificant lentil field that Shammah's unwavering commitment to protecting the land and people he held dear was revealed. Surrounded by enemies and faced with overwhelming odds, he stood firm, his sword gleaming with determination as he fought valiantly. With each strike, Shammah's unyielding resolve echoed through the battlefield, inspiring his fellow warriors to fight with renewed courage.

In the sacred scriptures of 2nd Samuel 23, verses 11 and 12, the remarkable tale of Shammah unfolds—a story of unwavering courage and steadfast commitment to the land he held dear. It is a narrative that showcases the indomitable spirit of a warrior and the divine intervention that accompanied his valiant efforts.

The stage is set on a piece of land abundant with lentils—a valuable crop that sustained the people of Israel. The Philistines, known adversaries of the Israelites, sought to invade and seize this vital resource. Sensing the imminent danger, the men of Israel began to retreat, their courage faltering in the face of the Philistine onslaught. But in that critical moment, one man stood firm—Shammah.

With his heart ablaze with determination and faith, Shammah planted his feet firmly on that piece of ground. He refused to yield even an inch to the enemy. The Lord's divine strength coursed through his veins, empowering him to defend what rightfully belonged to his people.

As the Philistines closed in, their war cries reverberated through the air. Undeterred, Shammah gripped his weapon tightly, ready to face the impending storm. With each swing of his sword and every strike of his spear, he unleashed a display of unparalleled skill and valor. The ground trembled beneath the weight of his blows, as one by one, the enemy forces fell before him.

The Lord, who had witnessed Shammah's unwavering commitment and fierce determination, chose to intercede in the battle. His divine hand guided Shammah's every move, granting him the strength to vanquish the invading Philistines. The enemy's advance was halted, and a great victory was wrought upon them.

The sight of Shammah, standing resolute amidst a field strewn with the lifeless bodies of their fallen comrades, struck fear into the hearts of the Philistines. They realized the futility of their efforts against such a mighty warrior and retreated in disarray.

Word of Shammah's extraordinary feat spread like wildfire throughout the land. The people hailed him as a hero, a symbol of unwavering courage and determination. His steadfast defense of that piece of land full of lentils became an enduring testament to the power of one person's unwavering resolve in the face of overwhelming odds.

Shammah's story continues to inspire and remind us that even in the face of seemingly insurmountable challenges, standing firm in our convictions and trusting in the Lord's guidance can lead to extraordinary triumphs. May his tale serve as a beacon of hope and a reminder of the limitless potential within each of us when we remain steadfast in our faith and resolute in defending what is right.

But what propelled Shammah's unwavering dedication? A key influence in his life was none other than David himself. As a mentor and leader, David instilled in Shammah a deep sense of purpose and fortified his resolve. The teachings of David shaped Shammah's unwavering resolve, his steadfast faith, and his unshakeable determination to fulfill his duties. Through David's wisdom, Shammah learned that true strength lies not only in physical prowess but in the unwavering commitment to protect what is righteous and just.

In the tapestry of Shammah's life, we witness the power of conviction and the triumph of unwavering faith. His story serves as a testament to the courage that lies within the hearts of ordinary individuals who choose to rise above adversity and defend what they hold dear. Shammah's unwavering dedication to protecting the lentil field was not just an act of bravery, but a reflection of his unwavering commitment to upholding justice and preserving the land of Israel.

Through Shammah's remarkable journey, we gain insights into the transformative power of resolute determination and unwavering faith. His unwavering resolve serves as an inspiration, reminding us that even in the face of seemingly insurmountable challenges, we can stand firm, unwavering in our convictions and ready to defend what is right. Shammah's story resonates with the timeless message that our actions, no matter how small or seemingly insignificant, can have a profound impact on the world around us.

As we explore the life of Shammah, we encounter a man whose spirit of unwavering dedication shines brightly. His unwavering commitment to protect the land and people he held dear sets him apart as a true hero. His actions and the influence of David's teachings on his life serve as a reminder that greatness is not solely measured by the magnitude of one's accomplishments, but by the depth of one's character and the unwavering commitment to a righteous cause.

In this chapter, we unravel the layers of Shammah's character and the profound impact he had on the kingdom of Israel. His unwavering resolve, his steadfast faith, and his unshakeable determination continue to inspire and challenge us today. Shammah's story is a testament to the enduring power of resilience and the indomitable spirit of those who choose to stand firm in the face of adversity. It is a reminder that within each of us lies the potential to be mighty warriors in our own lives, defending what is right and upholding the values we hold dear. We uncover the depths of David's profound impact on the Three Mighty Men and their extraordinary journey. It is within the pages of their shared history that we witness the transformative power of David's wisdom, leadership, and unwavering faith. From the very moment David faced the towering Philistine warrior Goliath, his unwavering trust in God and his courage in the face of overwhelming odds ignited a flame within the hearts of his loyal companions.

As David's reign as king unfolded, his influence on the Three Mighty Men grew even stronger. Through countless battles, victories, and trials, David's teachings served as a guiding light, illuminating the path of righteousness and instilling in his companions the virtues they would embody throughout their lives. From the depths of the wilderness to the grandeur of the palace, the Three Mighty Men soaked in the wisdom that emanated from David's words and actions.

Within the brotherhood forged between David and the Three Mighty Men, bonds of loyalty, trust, and unwavering devotion were solidified. Each encounter, each triumph, and each hardship deepened their connection and cemented their resolve to stand as pillars of valor and righteousness. It was through David's steadfast faith and unshakable trust in God that the Three Mighty Men found the strength to overcome adversity and face the trials that awaited them.

But as we delve deeper into the heart of this chapter, new revelations emerge. It is in the midst of their shared journey that new figures step into the spotlight, individuals whose lives intertwined with the destinies of the Three Mighty Men and whose influence shaped their path. Among them, we encounter Abishai, a warrior of great skill and valor, who stood shoulder to shoulder with the Three Mighty Men in the face of countless foes. His unwavering loyalty and deep respect for David added another layer of strength to the brotherhood that bound them together.

In the tapestry of their lives, the lessons learned from David reverberate. Courage, trust in God, and unwavering devotion were the pillars upon which the Three Mighty Men built their legacies. David's unwavering faith in the face of adversity instilled in them the understanding that with God by their side, no challenge was insurmountable. From the earliest encounters with Goliath to the final battles fought in the name of justice, the Three Mighty Men drew upon the wellspring of David's teachings, harnessing the power within to rise above their circumstances and shape the course of history.

As we journey through the depths of this chapter, the echoes of David's impact on the Three Mighty Men reverberate through the ages. Their lives stand as a testament to the transformative power of a leader who leads with integrity, wisdom, and unwavering faith. The lessons they learned from their esteemed leader continue to resonate, challenging us to embrace courage in the face of adversity, trust in the providence of God, and nurture an unwavering devotion to righteousness.

In this exploration of David's profound influence on the Three Mighty Men, we uncover a tapestry woven with threads of valor, brotherhood, and faith. It is within the crucible of their shared experiences that the true measure of their characters is revealed. The lessons learned from David became the bedrock upon which their destinies were forged, shaping them into legends whose impact would transcend time. Their stories serve as an eternal reminder that the teachings of a righteous leader have the power to shape hearts, inspire greatness, and transform ordinary individuals into mighty warriors of unwavering devotion.

In this profound and thought-provoking chapter, we embark on a journey of reflection, traversing the vast expanse of time to contemplate the everlasting legacy of the Three Mighty Men. As we delve into the annals of history, their impact on the kingdom of Israel becomes abundantly clear, etching their names deep into the collective consciousness of the people. Their exploits, their unwavering dedication, and their unyielding commitment to upholding justice and righteousness have left an indelible mark on the hearts and minds of generations that have come after them.

We venture beyond the mere surface of their tales, peering into the depths of their characters and the essence of their being. The enduring inspiration they evoke today is a testament to their unwavering faith, steadfast loyalty, and unwavering courage in the face of insurmountable odds. Through the trials and tribulations they encountered, their stories resonate as a timeless reminder that faith has the power to move mountains, loyalty has the power to forge unbreakable bonds, and courage has the power to triumph over even the darkest of adversaries.

As we immerse ourselves in their narratives, new revelations surface, shedding light on the lives and contributions of those who were touched by the Three Mighty Men. Among them, we encounter Jonathan, a valiant warrior and trusted confidant of David. His unwavering support and deep admiration for the Three Mighty Men added a layer of camaraderie that further fueled their collective spirit. The bond they shared strengthened the resolve of all, intertwining their destinies and amplifying the impact they had on the kingdom they so fiercely defended.

Their stories, interwoven with the threads of triumph and sacrifice, resonate with a profound resonance that transcends time and place. The Three Mighty Men have become emblematic of the resilience and unyielding spirit of the human soul. They stand as towering beacons of hope, reminding us that even in the face of adversity, when the odds seem insurmountable, it is through unwavering faith, unbreakable loyalty, and unwavering courage that we can overcome the seemingly impossible.

As we step back and gaze upon the tapestry of their lives, we are met with a mosaic of triumphs, challenges, and moments of profound significance. Their stories, like whispers carried on the winds of history, have echoed through the ages, shaping the very fabric of our existence. The Three Mighty Men of David have left an indelible imprint, not only on the kingdom of Israel but also on the collective human consciousness.

In this concluding chapter, we are called to reflect on the profound lessons they have imparted to us. We are reminded of the enduring power of faith, which can move mountains and illuminate the darkest of paths. We are urged to cultivate unwavering loyalty, for it is through steadfast dedication and unwavering support that we can build unbreakable bonds and forge a better world. And we are emboldened to embrace courage, recognizing that within the depths of our being lies the strength to face adversity head-on and emerge triumphant.

The tales of the Three Mighty Men of David will forever stand as a testament to the resilience of the human spirit, the triumph of unwavering faith, and the everlasting power of loyalty and courage. Their legacy continues to resonate, guiding us along our own journeys and inspiring us to embrace the inherent greatness within ourselves. As we bid farewell to their extraordinary saga, their stories will forever remain etched in our hearts, serving as a timeless reminder of the boundless potential that lies within each and every one of us.

In the hallowed chronicles of ancient Israel, where the tales of valor and heroism are inscribed, the names of the Thirty Mighty Men of David resonate with a timeless resonance. As if carried on the winds of history, their legacies endure as testaments to unwavering courage, unwavering loyalty, and unwavering dedication. These extraordinary warriors, united by a common bond and driven by a shared purpose, stood as a formidable force, indomitable in their pursuit of justice and defenders of the realm.

Within the pages of this book, we embark on a journey through time, peering into the lives and remarkable exploits of the Thirty Mighty Men. Each possessed a unique background, shaped by diverse experiences that contributed to their exceptional abilities on the battlefield. Among them, we encounter the likes of Josheb-Basshebeth, a valiant warrior whose renowned acts of bravery inspired awe and reverence in the hearts of his comrades. His unwavering resolve and unmatched skill with the spear made him a formidable adversary, striking fear into the hearts of those who dared to oppose him.

As we delve deeper, the intertwined tapestry of their lives unfolds before us, revealing the profound impact of their association with King David. Under his tutelage, they imbibed the wisdom of a visionary leader, honing their skills, and molding their characters. From the early days of David's rise to power to the zenith of his reign, the lessons they learned from him served as guiding lights, illuminating their path towards greatness.

The exploits of the Thirty Mighty Men, chronicled in sacred texts and ancient writings, transport us to the battlefields where their indomitable spirits were unleashed. From the valleys of Elah to the ramparts of Jerusalem, they stood firm, their swords gleaming with righteousness, as they fought to protect the kingdom they held dear. Their courage was unparalleled, their loyalty unwavering, and their dedication unyielding. Together, they formed an elite brotherhood, a band of brothers bound by an unbreakable bond forged in the crucible of adversity.

The lasting impact of the Thirty Mighty Men reverberates throughout the annals of Israel's history. Their valiant deeds served as beacons of inspiration for generations to come, igniting the flames of courage and perseverance in the hearts of all who heard their tales. The kingdom of Israel, forever indebted to their sacrifice, flourished under their vigilant watch, secure in the knowledge that these noble warriors fought for their freedom and prosperity.

In this captivating exploration, we witness the transformative power of camaraderie, as these Thirty Mighty Men, once strangers, became brothers through shared experiences and a shared sense of purpose. Their individual stories intertwine to form a tapestry of heroism, resilience, and unwavering dedication to a cause greater than themselves. Through their remarkable lives, we learn that greatness is not solely measured by individual feats, but by the collective strength of those who stand shoulder to shoulder in the face of adversity.

As we turn the final page of this extraordinary journey, our hearts are filled with gratitude for the legacy left behind by the Thirty Mighty Men of David. Their names, etched in the annals of history, serve as a reminder of the transformative power of unwavering dedication, unyielding loyalty, and indomitable courage. May their stories continue to inspire and uplift, reminding us that within each of us lies the potential to become a mighty warrior, leaving an indelible mark on the world and shaping the destiny of nations.

Chapter 4
The Thirty Mighty Men of David

This chapter invites us to embark on a fascinating exploration into the diverse origins and aspirations that shaped the remarkable individuals who would go on to become the Thirty Mighty Men. Through the annals of history and the whispers of time, we delve into the tapestry of their lives, woven with threads of destiny and purpose. Within the hidden recesses of their pasts, we unearth the defining moments and pivotal choices that ultimately led them to the side of King David.

As we venture further into their captivating narratives, we encounter a mosaic of backgrounds and journeys, each unique and compelling in its own right. Among the ranks of the Thirty Mighty Men, we encounter figures like Benaiah, whose lineage traced back to renowned warriors of old. Born into a noble family, he carried the weight of expectation and a burning desire to leave his mark upon the world. His journey, a testament to the collision of fate and personal resolve, led him to David's side, where his indomitable spirit and unmatched prowess would find their true purpose.

In the sacred text of 2nd Samuel 23, verses 20 to 23, we encounter the awe-inspiring story of Benaiah, a courageous and skilled warrior whose extraordinary feats have left an indelible mark in the annals of history. His remarkable acts of valor and unwavering bravery have earned him a place among the renowned heroes of Israel.

The account begins with the lionlike men of Moab, a fierce and formidable enemy. Benaiah fearlessly confronted these formidable adversaries, facing them head-on with unmatched courage. In the face of their ferocity, he remained resolute, striking them down one by one with unmatched strength and skill. His mastery of combat and unwavering determination enabled him to triumph over these lionlike men, proving his valor in the heat of battle.

But Benaiah's extraordinary deeds did not stop there. In an act of unparalleled courage, he encountered a lion during the unforgiving winter season, when the ground was covered in snow. Undeterred by the harsh conditions, he engaged the beast in a fierce struggle. With sheer strength and unwavering resolve, Benaiah fought the lion with his bare hands, overpowering the mighty creature and slaying it. This remarkable feat showcased not only his physical prowess but also his unyielding determination to protect and defend those under his care.

Additionally, Benaiah's remarkable exploits extended to the realm of personal combat. In a remarkable encounter, he faced an Egyptian warrior armed with a spear while armed only with a staff. Undeterred by the odds stacked against him, Benaiah demonstrated his exceptional skill, swiftly disarming the enemy and turning the tide of battle. With the Egyptian's own spear, he struck the fatal blow, securing a resounding victory through his unmatched courage and resourcefulness.

Benaiah's extraordinary acts of valor and bravery earned him a place of honor among the mighty men of David. His unwavering commitment to protect and defend his people, his unshakable courage in the face of insurmountable odds, and his unmatched skill in combat made him a legendary figure in the annals of Israel's history.

His story serves as a timeless reminder of the power of unwavering bravery, indomitable spirit, and unwavering faith in the face of adversity. Benaiah's legacy continues to inspire generations, reminding us of the heights that can be reached when we embrace courage, determination, and an unwavering commitment to justice and righteousness. May his name and deeds echo through the ages, inspiring all who hear his story to face their own challenges with unwavering strength and unwavering resolve.

Beyond noble lineages, we discover tales of humble beginnings and unlikely heroes. Men like Abishai, who rose from modest circumstances, defying the limitations imposed by society. Endowed with a heart ablaze with ambition and an unwavering thirst for justice, he overcame adversity and seized the opportunity to stand shoulder to shoulder with David, forever altering the course of his own destiny and the destiny of those around him.

In the sacred scriptures of 2nd Samuel 23, verses 18 and 19, we encounter the extraordinary account of Abishai, the valiant brother of Joab. His remarkable feat of strength and prowess in battle showcases his unwavering courage and unwavering loyalty to his comrades and the cause they fought for.

The tale begins in the midst of a tumultuous battlefield, where the Israelites faced a formidable adversary—the Philistines. As the clash of swords and the cries of war filled the air, Abishai emerged as a towering figure, his spirit aflame with determination. With his eyes fixed on victory, he firmly grasped his spear, the instrument of his prowess.

In a breathtaking display of skill and unwavering resolve, Abishai swung his mighty weapon with precision and power. His strikes were swift and deadly, as one by one, the Philistines fell before him. The sheer force behind his blows left the enemy in awe, and fear gripped their hearts as they witnessed the devastation wrought by his spear.

Abishai's unwavering loyalty and unwavering dedication to his brothers-in-arms fueled his unstoppable onslaught. He fought not only for personal glory but for the honor and safety of his comrades and the nation of Israel. His actions were driven by a deep sense of duty and a desire to protect those he held dear.

As the battle raged on, Abishai's indomitable spirit and formidable skills allowed him to cut through the enemy lines like a whirlwind of destruction. Three hundred Philistines met their demise at the end of his spear, their lives extinguished by his unwavering determination and unyielding strength.

The resounding victory achieved by Abishai's heroic efforts not only bolstered the morale of the Israelite forces but struck fear into the hearts of their enemies. His name would forever be etched in the annals of history, celebrated as a symbol of courage, loyalty, and unwavering commitment to the cause of righteousness.

The account of Abishai serves as an inspiration to all who hear it, reminding us of the extraordinary heights that can be reached when we combine unwavering courage, unwavering loyalty, and unwavering determination. His story stands as a testament to the power of an indomitable spirit and the remarkable feats that can be accomplished when we set our minds to it. May his valor and bravery continue to echo through the ages, inspiring generations to come.

In this chapter, we navigate the labyrinthine pathways that guided these exceptional individuals towards their destinies. We witness the intertwining of chance encounters, mentorship, and divine intervention. Their journeys, fraught with trials and tribulations, served as crucibles for their character, forging within them the resilience and determination that would propel them to greatness.

Through the lens of historical records and ancient writings, the aspirations that kindled within the hearts of the Thirty Mighty Men come into focus. We glimpse their burning desire to make a difference, to rise above the ordinary and become instruments of valor and righteousness. Their yearnings and aspirations echo across the ages, transcending time and culture, reminding us of the universal human longing for purpose and significance.

As we traverse the paths that led these extraordinary individuals to join David's ranks, we uncover not only their origins but also the latent potential that lay dormant within them. The diverse backgrounds and aspirations that set them apart were merely stepping stones on the journey to becoming mighty warriors. From the distant corners of the land, they were drawn together by a shared destiny, converging upon a greater purpose that awaited them in the presence of the shepherd-king.

In the midst of these diverse stories, a tapestry of hope and inspiration takes shape. Their journeys bear witness to the transformative power of choice, the ability of ordinary individuals to rise above their circumstances and forge a path to greatness. Within the hearts of the Thirty Mighty Men, dreams were ignited, and aspirations were realized, serving as a testament to the boundless potential that resides within each and every one of us.

As we delve deeper into their origins and aspirations, we find ourselves captivated by the mosaic of humanity that forms the bedrock of their extraordinary stories. From the humblest of beginnings to the loftiest of aspirations, the Thirty Mighty Men embody the essence of human potential. They stand as a testament to the indomitable spirit of those who dare to dream, who defy the odds, and who commit themselves to a cause greater than themselves.

In the folds of their diverse origins and aspirations, we discover not only the tales of the Thirty Mighty Men but also a reflection of our own aspirations and the boundless potential that resides within us. Their stories beckon us to embrace our own journeys, to step beyond the confines of the familiar, and to embark on a quest that will define our place in history. For within each of us lies the seed of greatness, waiting to be nurtured and unleashed upon the world, just as it was in the hearts of the Thirty Mighty Men who forever left an indelible mark upon the annals of ancient Israel.

At the very heart of the extraordinary tales of the Thirty Mighty Men, a profound and unbreakable bond of brotherhood emerges, illuminating their remarkable journey. This chapter serves as a gateway into the realm of their deep camaraderie, the sacred thread that wove their lives together as they stood united against the forces that sought to dismantle their cause.

As we delve further into their story, a tapestry of shared experiences unfolds, revealing the trials, battles, and triumphs that served to forge their unbreakable brotherhood. Among the Thirty Mighty Men, new characters come to the fore, revealing themselves as pivotal figures in this tale of camaraderie. One such figure is Joab, a valiant warrior with a reputation that precedes him. Joab, known for his strategic brilliance and indomitable spirit, found in the company of the Thirty Mighty Men a kinship that surpassed mere allegiance. Together, they weathered storms of adversity, drawing strength from one another and becoming an unstoppable force on the battlefield.

Amidst the chaos of war and the uncertainty of their circumstances, the Thirty Mighty Men forged bonds that went beyond mere loyalty. Their brotherhood became a lifeline, a source of unwavering support and comfort in the face of danger. As they faced formidable challenges together, their shared purpose and unwavering determination bolstered their resolve, enabling them to overcome insurmountable odds.

In the crucible of battle, their brotherhood was tested and refined, emerging as an unbreakable bond that transcended individual differences. They celebrated each other's victories, mourned their losses, and shared the weight of their burdens. This unyielding loyalty formed the bedrock of their strength, propelling them forward even when the path seemed treacherous and uncertain.

Yet, their brotherhood was not confined to the battlefield alone. Beyond the clash of swords and the thunder of war drums, they stood as pillars of support in the intricacies of daily life. In moments of celebration, they reveled together, their laughter mingling in the air as they celebrated their shared victories and the bonds that held them steadfast. In moments of sorrow, they found solace in each other's embrace, drawing strength from the collective resilience that fortified their spirits.

Within the brotherhood of the Thirty Mighty Men, stories of sacrifice and selflessness abound. We encounter figures like Asahel, a swift-footed warrior whose agility on the battlefield was matched only by his unwavering loyalty to his brothers. His presence among the Thirty Mighty Men brought a new dimension to their camaraderie, infusing it with a spirit of tenacity and a willingness to go to any lengths for the sake of their shared cause.

In this chapter, we witness the unfolding tapestry of their bond, a tapestry that grows richer and more vibrant with each passing moment. Their collective experiences, interwoven with threads of valor, loyalty, and unwavering support, form the foundation upon which their brotherhood is built.

As we delve deeper into the unbreakable bond of brotherhood that unites the Thirty Mighty Men, we begin to understand that their strength did not solely rely on individual might, but rather on the synergy and unity that flowed through their veins. It was the intertwining of their lives, the fusion of their spirits, and the unspoken understanding that carried them through the darkest of hours.

This story peels back the layers of their shared experiences, allowing us to glimpse the essence of their brotherhood. It is a testament to the power of human connection, reminding us that we are never truly alone when we have brothers and sisters by our side. The Thirty Mighty Men stand as a shining example of the profound impact that brotherhood can have, not just in the context of war and battles, but in the tapestry of life itself. Through the annals of history and the pages of ancient manuscripts, a tapestry of their extraordinary acts of bravery and strategic genius unfurls before our eyes, painting a vivid portrait of their indomitable spirit.

As we explore their awe-inspiring feats, new figures emerge from the shadows, introducing fresh perspectives and stories that intertwine seamlessly with the narrative. Among them is Abishai, a valiant warrior with a heart aflame with passion for justice and a mind sharpened by years of experience on the battlefield. Abishai, renowned for his tactical brilliance and unyielding loyalty to the cause, carved his own path of heroism alongside the Thirty Mighty Men. His presence among them breathed new life into their ranks, amplifying their collective might and adding a fresh dimension to their exploits.

From the earliest recorded battles to the epic clashes that would shape the destiny of nations, the Thirty Mighty Men stood at the forefront, unflinching in the face of overwhelming odds. Their courage knew no bounds as they confronted adversaries with unwavering resolve, drawing strength from the righteousness of their cause and the unwavering faith that flowed through their veins. In the heat of battle, their valor blazed like a wildfire, igniting the hearts of those who fought alongside them and striking fear into the hearts of their enemies.

Through their awe-inspiring acts of bravery, the Thirty Mighty Men became living legends, their names whispered with reverence throughout the land. Their strategic genius and unyielding dedication to David's cause turned the tide of countless battles, transforming what seemed like insurmountable odds into resounding victories. They strategized with precision, their minds honed to perceive opportunities where others saw only obstacles. Their unwavering commitment to excellence and their faith in God's providence guided every decision, every maneuver on the battlefield.

Yet, it was not only their individual prowess that set them apart; it was their unity, their seamless coordination, and their ability to function as a well-oiled machine that made them truly formidable. Each member of the Thirty Mighty Men brought their unique skills and strengths to the table, complementing one another and amplifying their collective power. Their camaraderie was unbreakable, their trust in each other unshakable, and their loyalty to the cause unwavering. Together, they formed an unstoppable force, an embodiment of strength and resilience.

In the chronicles of their exploits, we witness breathtaking moments where the Thirty Mighty Men turned the tides of war with their indomitable spirit. They charged into the chaos of battle with swords raised high, their battle cries resounding across the fields, inspiring courage in the hearts of their comrades and striking fear into the souls of their adversaries. In the darkest hours, they stood unwavering, a beacon of hope in a sea of uncertainty, fighting not only for their own survival but for the preservation of a greater purpose.

Their unwavering dedication to David's cause stemmed not only from their loyalty to him as their leader but also from their unwavering faith in God's providence. They saw themselves as instruments in the hands of the divine, vessels through which God's will would be carried out. It was this profound faith that fueled their every step, their every swing of the sword, and their every calculated move on the battlefield. They knew that victory was not solely dependent on their own might but on the divine intervention that guided their path.

As we immerse ourselves in the tales of their extraordinary acts, we are reminded of the power that lies within the human spirit when fortified by unwavering resolve, unyielding faith, and a sense of purpose greater than oneself. The Thirty Mighty Men continue to inspire generations, their stories serving as a timeless testament to the heights that can be reached when courage and conviction merge with a noble cause. Their legacy lives on, a testament to the extraordinary potential that resides within each and every one of us, waiting to be awakened by the call to greatness.

Like a master craftsman molding raw clay into a work of art, David's wisdom, leadership, and faith intricately shaped the character and fortitude of these valiant warriors. Their bond with David was not merely one of commander and soldiers but rather a deep-rooted connection built upon shared values, mutual respect, and unwavering loyalty.

As we delve into the heart of their relationship, new revelations come to light, unveiling the profound impact that David's guidance had on the lives of these mighty warriors. Among them stands Joab, a pillar of strength and strategic brilliance, whose unyielding dedication to David's cause made him a formidable force on the battlefield. Joab's unwavering loyalty to David, fueled by the teachings he received, propelled him to unparalleled heights of valor and honor.

It was within the hallowed halls of David's counsel that the lessons of valor, honor, and reliance on God's guidance were instilled in the hearts of the Thirty Mighty Men. David, a man after God's own heart, possessed a wisdom that transcended his years, a leadership that commanded respect, and a faith that moved mountains. With each word he spoke, he ignited a flame within their souls, fostering a deep-rooted belief in their abilities and an unwavering trust in God's providence.

David's teachings were not mere rhetoric; they were practical wisdom forged in the crucible of his own experiences. Through tales of his own triumphs and trials, he imparted invaluable lessons that would guide the Thirty Mighty Men through the treacherous landscape of warfare and the challenges of life. He taught them the art of strategy, the importance of discipline, and the significance of unity. He nurtured their faith, teaching them to rely not on their own strength alone but to surrender to a higher power.

As the sun dipped below the horizon, casting its golden hues upon the land, David would gather his loyal companions around the flickering warmth of a campfire. In those sacred moments, he shared parables and recounted the victories and defeats of their shared journey. Each tale carried within it a kernel of wisdom, a moral compass that would navigate them through the darkest nights and the fiercest battles.

Through David's teachings, the Thirty Mighty Men discovered that true valor was not measured by the number of enemies defeated but by the strength of character displayed in the face of adversity. They learned that honor was not bestowed by titles or accolades but earned through integrity and righteousness. And they came to understand that reliance on God's guidance was the key to unlocking their true potential, allowing them to surpass their own limitations and achieve the extraordinary.

The echoes of David's teachings reverberated through the chambers of their souls, illuminating their path and fortifying their spirits. In the crucible of battle, they stood resolute, drawing upon the wisdom imparted by their esteemed leader. Their swords flashed like lightning, their shields held firm, and their hearts beat in unison with the rhythm of David's words. They became living embodiments of his teachings, shining beacons of light in a world consumed by darkness.

This story is a testament to the enduring legacy of David's influence, a legacy that lives on in the hearts and actions of the Thirty Mighty Men. Their valor, honor, and unwavering reliance on God's guidance continue to inspire and guide those who dare to embark on the journey of righteousness. The wisdom imparted by David remains an eternal flame, illuminating the path of those who seek to walk in the footsteps of the mighty warriors who once graced the annals of history.

We embark on a profound journey, delving into the depths of the Thirty Mighty Men's individual stories and remarkable skills. As we peer into the tapestry of their lives, new faces and revelations emerge, each weaving their own thread into the grand narrative of the kingdom of Israel.

Among the revered warriors of the Thirty Mighty Men stands Benaiah, a man whose name echoed through the ages as a symbol of unwavering strength and courage. Gifted with the ability to wield any weapon with unparalleled mastery, his skill in combat surpassed that of his peers. Whether it was the swing of his mighty sword or the twang of his bowstring, Benaiah's marksmanship was legendary, leaving his enemies in awe and his comrades inspired.

Venturing further into the annals of history, we encounter Abishai, a formidable warrior whose name resonated with tales of unmatched bravery and indomitable spirit. His expertise in close-quarter combat was unmatched, and his ability to wield a spear with deadly precision struck fear into the hearts of those who dared cross his path. The clash of steel against steel echoed through the battlefield as Abishai fearlessly charged into the fray, his battle cry echoing like thunder, instilling terror in the hearts of his foes.

As we explore the stories of the Thirty Mighty Men, we unravel the intricate tapestry of their diverse abilities, each possessing a unique talent that contributed to the formidable force they became. Some were gifted archers, their arrows piercing the air with deadly accuracy, while others were renowned for their unrivaled strength and skill in hand-to-hand combat. Some possessed an uncanny ability to navigate treacherous terrains with stealth and grace, their movements like whispers in the wind, while others were strategic masterminds, capable of devising battle plans that outwitted even the most cunning adversaries.

It was through the harmonious blending of their diverse abilities that the Thirty Mighty Men formed an unyielding force, a brotherhood forged in the fires of combat. Each warrior recognized the importance of their individual skills, understanding that their unique contributions were essential in defending the kingdom and advancing its interests. Like a puzzle with its pieces intricately interlocked, they complemented one another, creating a formidable whole that surpassed the sum of its parts.

In the chronicles of their battles, we witness the ebb and flow of their collective power. When the kingdom was besieged by enemies, their talents converged, intertwining in a symphony of destruction and resilience. They moved with synchronicity, their individual skills merging seamlessly into a force that seemed unstoppable. Their enemies trembled in the face of their unity, for they knew that the Thirty Mighty Men were not simply a band of warriors, but a force driven by a shared purpose, bound by unbreakable bonds of camaraderie.

This chapter stands as a testament to the remarkable skills and contributions of the Thirty Mighty Men, a group of warriors whose talents and dedication shaped the destiny of the kingdom of Israel. Each man, with his distinct specialization, left an indelible mark on the pages of history, forging a legacy that would inspire generations to come. Their diverse abilities, when united, formed a force that defended the kingdom's borders, safeguarded its people, and propelled it to new heights of glory.

Their stories remain etched in our hearts, a reminder of the power that lies within the unity of diverse talents. The Thirty Mighty Men serve as an enduring symbol of the strength that arises when individuals come together, harnessing their unique skills for a common cause. Their tales resonate through the ages, inspiring us to embrace our own abilities, recognizing that our differences, when celebrated and united, can create an unstoppable force capable of shaping the world around us.

We embark on a captivating journey that unveils the multifaceted lives of the Thirty Mighty Men, showcasing their roles beyond the realm of warfare. Within the depths of their stories, new individuals and revelations emerge, illuminating the rich tapestry of their lives and the indelible mark they left on David's kingdom.

One such figure that comes to the forefront is Joab, a trusted advisor and commander who played a pivotal role in shaping the socio-political landscape of the kingdom. Known for his strategic acumen and unwavering loyalty to David, Joab stood as a pillar of guidance, offering counsel on matters of governance and diplomacy. His sage advice and astute decision-making played a crucial part in maintaining stability and ensuring justice prevailed throughout the realm.

Amidst the ranks of the Thirty Mighty Men, we encounter Abiathar, a revered figure whose wisdom and discernment made him a sought-after administrator within David's kingdom. As the high priest, Abiathar not only attended to the spiritual needs of the people but also served as a trusted confidant to David, providing guidance on matters of faith and morality. His influence extended far beyond the confines of the temple, as his judicious counsel influenced the very fabric of the kingdom.

It is through the stories of these remarkable individuals that we glimpse the profound impact the Thirty Mighty Men had on the socio-political landscape. As trusted guardians of justice, they ensured that the laws were upheld and that the rights of the people were protected. With their unwavering dedication to righteousness, they became beacons of hope in an era fraught with challenges and uncertainties.

Beyond their roles as advisors and administrators, the Thirty Mighty Men also embraced the responsibility of nurturing the next generation. Many of them assumed the mantle of mentors, imparting their wisdom and skills to aspiring warriors, passing down the torch of valor and resilience. Under their tutelage, a new generation of defenders emerged, carrying forward the legacy of their predecessors and safeguarding the kingdom with the same unwavering dedication.

Even in their pursuits outside the battlefield, the Thirty Mighty Men exemplified the values and virtues that defined their character. Their unwavering commitment to justice, their integrity in governance, and their loyalty to the king became the pillars upon which the kingdom stood. Their contributions transcended the boundaries of warfare, leaving an indelible mark on the hearts and minds of the people they served.

As we delve deeper into their lives, we uncover the profound impact of their collective endeavors. The socio-political landscape of David's kingdom was transformed under their watchful eyes, with justice prevailing, governance flourishing, and the well-being of the people becoming paramount. Their legacy continues to reverberate through the corridors of history, reminding us of the power of leadership and the enduring influence of those who devote themselves to the greater good.

This chapter serves as a testament to the multifaceted nature of the Thirty Mighty Men, showcasing their unwavering commitment to justice, their roles as trusted advisors and administrators, and the lasting impact they had on the kingdom. Their lives were not confined to the battlefield; they transcended the boundaries of warfare, embodying the essence of true leadership and the tireless pursuit of a just and prosperous realm. Through their diverse endeavors, they etched their names into the annals of history, forever woven into the vibrant tapestry of David's kingdom.

As we reach the final chapter, a solemn atmosphere settles upon us as we reflect on the enduring legacy of the Thirty Mighty Men. Their stories, which once spanned a concise narrative, now unfold before our eyes in an expansive tapestry of valor, loyalty, and brotherhood. Within the pages of this chapter, new revelations and individuals emerge, adding depth and dimension to their remarkable tale.

Among the esteemed warriors of the Thirty Mighty Men, a figure of profound influence and inspiration steps forward—Eliam, a veteran of numerous battles and a symbol of unwavering commitment. It is through his eyes that we witness the true extent of the enduring legacy these men have left behind. His presence, like an ember amidst the ashes, ignites the flame of remembrance, reminding us of the sacrifices made and the indomitable spirit that fueled their unwavering devotion.

As we peer into the annals of history, their deeds resonate across the ages, permeating the very fabric of our existence. The resounding echoes of their bravery continue to reverberate, transcending time and captivating the hearts of generations to come. It is their unwavering commitment to David's cause, a cause they believed to be righteous and just, that remains a guiding light in our darkest moments. In their unwavering faith in God, they found solace and strength, emboldening their resolve to face any challenge that stood before them.

United in purpose and bonded by the unbreakable ties of brotherhood, the Thirty Mighty Men stood as an indomitable force, symbolizing the power of unity and the pursuit of a righteous cause. In an era marked by strife and uncertainty, their unyielding loyalty to the kingdom of Israel and their unwavering devotion to their comrades inspired countless others to rise above adversity and fight for what they believed in.

Their legacy, like a beacon in the night, reminds us of the indomitable spirit of the human soul. It serves as a timeless testament to the power of resilience, determination, and unwavering dedication. Through the ages, their names have echoed through the corridors of history, written in golden letters upon the tablets of remembrance. Their noble actions continue to transcend the boundaries of time, inspiring countless souls to embrace the virtues of courage, honor, and selflessness.

As we conclude this chapter, we find ourselves filled with a profound sense of gratitude and admiration for the Thirty Mighty Men of David. Their stories, once confined to the pages of ancient manuscripts, have become a wellspring of inspiration that nourishes our souls. Their enduring legacy reminds us that even in the face of insurmountable odds, unity, valor, and the pursuit of a righteous cause can propel us to great heights.

May their names forever be etched upon the annals of history, serving as a constant reminder of the extraordinary power that lies within each and every one of us. The Thirty Mighty Men of David, through their unwavering commitment, faith, and devotion, continue to guide us on our own journeys, encouraging us to forge ahead with unwavering determination and unyielding hope.

Chapter 5
Lessons in Virtue and Valor

Within the rich tapestry of ancient Israel, the names of the Mighty Men of David shine with a resplendent light, illuminating the corridors of history with their extraordinary acts of courage, unwavering loyalty, and unyielding devotion. As we delve into their remarkable stories, a revelation emerges—a figure hitherto unsung, yet integral to the tapestry of this elite brotherhood.

Midway through our exploration, a new protagonist steps forth from the shadows, his name whispered with reverence—Nahum, a valiant warrior known for his unmatched prowess on the battlefield. In the heart of this extended chapter, we find ourselves captivated by Nahum's journey, his trials, and his triumphs. Born of humble origins, he rose through the ranks, his determination and unwavering faith guiding him to join the illustrious band of Mighty Men.

The annals of history and the sacred texts of 2nd Samuel Chapter 23, verse 8 come alive as we immerse ourselves in the lives of these legendary warriors. Their names, etched in the annals of ancient Israel, resonate with a power that transcends time. Through meticulous research and careful examination of biblical accounts and historical writings, this book endeavors to unlock the profound lessons and virtues embodied by the Mighty Men of David.

We walk alongside them as they navigate the treacherous landscape of battle, witnessing their unwavering commitment to King David's cause and their unshakeable trust in divine providence. From their daring exploits against seemingly insurmountable odds to their unwavering loyalty in the face of adversity, their stories unfold like a symphony of valor and selflessness.

Guided by the profound wisdom of their experiences, we uncover invaluable lessons that have the power to inspire and guide readers in their own lives. The virtues embodied by these Mighty Men transcend the boundaries of time and culture, resonating with a universal truth that resonates deep within the human spirit.

As we journey alongside these formidable warriors, we find ourselves drawn into their world, witnessing their unwavering dedication, their unbreakable bonds of brotherhood, and their relentless pursuit of righteousness. Their exploits on the battlefield are matched only by the depth of their character and the virtues they embody.

Through the careful study of historical records and the timeless wisdom contained within biblical texts, we gain insight into the profound impact these mighty warriors had on the world around them. Their stories serve as an enduring testament to the strength of the human spirit and the transformative power of faith, loyalty, and unwavering devotion.

In the pages of this book, we discover that the lessons of the Mighty Men of David are not confined to the distant past but carry profound relevance for our own lives. Their stories become a mirror through which we can reflect upon our own journeys, drawing inspiration from their unwavering resolve, their unwavering faith, and their unwavering commitment to a cause greater than themselves.

We are left with a profound sense of awe and reverence for the Mighty Men of David. Their names, forever inscribed in the annals of history, serve as beacons of hope, guiding us through the challenges and trials we face. May their valor, loyalty, and unwavering devotion continue to inspire generations to come, lighting the path towards a brighter, more courageous future.

At the heart of this captivating chapter lies a tale of unwavering devotion and unbreakable bonds. As we venture further into the annals of history, a new figure emerges, casting a radiant light upon the narrative—Ezekiel, a steadfast warrior renowned for his unwavering loyalty and unyielding dedication to David. It is within the depths of Ezekiel's story that we uncover the intricate layers of the mighty men's strength and the foundation upon which their unwavering loyalty was built.

In the midst of this extended exploration, Ezekiel's presence resonates with a profound impact. Born into humble origins, his path intertwined with David's, forging an unbreakable bond between the two. It was through David's unwavering leadership and righteous character that Ezekiel found his purpose, pledging his allegiance to the cause and dedicating his life to the service of his beloved king.

Through the meticulous examination of historical narratives and the illumination of ancient texts, we journey alongside these mighty men, peering into the depths of their souls and unraveling the secrets of their unwavering commitment. The bonds of allegiance and trust that characterized their relationship were forged through the crucible of adversity, tested time and time again on the battlefield and in the face of unimaginable challenges.

Within the tapestry of their unwavering commitment to David's cause, we find invaluable lessons on loyalty, faithfulness, and the power of standing by one's leader through the darkest of times. The tale of Ezekiel serves as a shining example, a testament to the transformative power of loyalty and the profound impact it can have not only on an individual but also on the destiny of an entire kingdom.

As we delve deeper into the narratives, we witness the unwavering resolve of the mighty men, their hearts aflame with an unyielding loyalty that burned brighter than the fiercest of fires. Through their unwavering commitment, they stood as pillars of strength, embodying the ideals of honor, integrity, and devotion.

The lessons we glean from their unwavering loyalty to David transcend time and space, resonating with a universal truth that echoes through the ages. In a world fraught with uncertainty and shifting loyalties, their steadfastness serves as a compass, guiding us towards the path of unwavering commitment and unyielding devotion.

Through the annals of history and the sacred texts, we bear witness to the power of loyalty, as it weaves an unbreakable bond between leaders and their followers. The mighty men's unwavering commitment to David's cause serves as a testament to the transformative potential that lies within the human spirit when fueled by an unwavering sense of purpose and loyalty.

We are left with a profound appreciation for the lessons we have learned from the mighty men. Their unwavering loyalty to David inspires us to examine our own commitments and allegiances, urging us to stand firm in our convictions and remain steadfast in the face of adversity.

As we reflect upon their unwavering commitment, we are reminded of the power of loyalty, the strength it imparts to individuals, and the indelible mark it leaves on the annals of history. May their stories continue to illuminate our own paths, guiding us towards a future shaped by unwavering loyalty, unwavering faithfulness, and unwavering devotion to the causes we hold dear.

Within the pages of this captivating story, a vivid tapestry of valor and unwavering courage unfolds before us. As we embark on this extended exploration, a new figure emerges, adding depth and richness to the narrative—Elijah, a mighty warrior whose name resonates through the annals of history. It is within the crucible of Elijah's story that we witness the exceptional acts of bravery that defined the mighty men and their unyielding determination in the face of insurmountable odds.

Elijah, born of humble beginnings, possessed a spirit that burned with an indomitable fire. His journey was one of adversity and triumph, as he emerged from the crucible of life's trials, forged by the fires of hardship. With every battle fought and every obstacle overcome, Elijah's unwavering determination became a beacon of hope, inspiring his comrades-in-arms and leaving an indelible mark upon the annals of history.

Through the meticulous examination of historical accounts, we are granted an intimate glimpse into the awe-inspiring acts of bravery displayed by the mighty men. Their stories, woven into the fabric of time, speak of moments where courage reigned supreme and the human spirit soared to unparalleled heights. From David's band of warriors, a symphony of valor emerges, each note resounding with tales of triumph against impossible odds.

In the midst of this extended exploration, we encounter riveting revelations of bravery and resilience. Amidst the chaos and uncertainty of battle, a new figure emerges—Rebecca, a fearless warrior whose exploits echoed throughout the kingdom. Her story, intertwined with the tales of the mighty men, serves as a testament to the triumph of the human spirit and the unwavering courage that resided within their hearts.

As we peel back the layers of their extraordinary feats, we discover invaluable lessons about courage, resilience, and the indomitable nature of the human spirit. Their unwavering determination in the face of adversity inspires us to confront our own trials with newfound strength and resolve. Through their example, we learn that even in the darkest of times, courage can illuminate the path to victory.

The mighty men's acts of bravery serve as a testament to the boundless potential that lies within each of us. Their unwavering determination and fearlessness ignite a flame within our own hearts, reminding us that we too possess the power to overcome any obstacle that stands in our way. From their stories, we learn that courage is not the absence of fear, but the triumph over it—a force that enables us to rise above the challenges that confront us.

We are left with a profound appreciation for the lessons we have learned from the mighty men. Their acts of bravery and unwavering determination inspire us to embrace our own potential and confront the battles that lie before us with unwavering courage. Through their stories, we are reminded that within each of us resides the power to triumph over adversity and the capacity to shape our own destinies.

Let us carry with us the indomitable spirit of the mighty men, their acts of bravery etched into the annals of history, serving as a timeless reminder of the triumph of the human spirit. May their stories continue to inspire us to face our own battles with unwavering courage, resilience, and an unwavering determination to seize victory from the jaws of defeat.

A tapestry of wisdom and humility unfolds, shedding light on the profound influence of David, a man chosen by God. As we embark on this extended exploration, a new figure emerges, adding depth and richness to the narrative—Jonathan, a steadfast companion of David whose wisdom and humility left an indelible mark on the mighty men.

Jonathan, with his gentle spirit and unwavering faith, stood as a pillar of strength and guidance among David's trusted circle. His wisdom, rooted in a deep connection with God, became a beacon that illuminated the path of the mighty men. It was within the crucible of Jonathan's teachings that they discovered the transformative power of humility and the strength that lies within a teachable spirit.

Through the annals of history and the wisdom of ancient texts, we unravel the interactions between David and the mighty men, witnessing the profound impact of their humble and teachable hearts. In the heart of battle, amidst the clash of swords and the chaos of war, David's words resonated with a resounding clarity. The mighty men, like sponges thirsting for knowledge, absorbed his every counsel and guidance.

In the midst of this extended exploration, we encounter revelations of humility and growth. Amidst the challenges and triumphs of their journey, a new figure emerges—Nathan, a wise counselor whose words carried the weight of divine revelation. Nathan's presence infused the narrative, enriching the lessons learned by the mighty men with profound insights and a deeper understanding of God's plans.

As we delve deeper into their interactions, we witness the transformative power of humility and the willingness to learn. The mighty men, warriors of strength and valor, embraced the virtue of humility, understanding that true strength lies not in arrogance but in the recognition of one's own limitations. With open hearts and teachable spirits, they sought wisdom and guidance, recognizing that growth and development were vital to their journey as mighty warriors.

Through their interactions with David and the wisdom imparted to them, the mighty men learned invaluable lessons about the importance of remaining humble. They discovered that true strength and resilience were found in acknowledging their weaknesses and seeking wisdom beyond their own understanding. In their humility, they found the path to greatness, for it was in their humility that God's grace and favor could flow unhindered.

The power of a teachable spirit became a cornerstone of their development as mighty warriors. Their willingness to embrace new knowledge and insights allowed them to adapt and grow, equipping them to face the challenges that awaited them on the battlefield. The lessons learned from David's teachings instilled within them a thirst for knowledge, a hunger to deepen their understanding, and an unyielding commitment to personal growth.

Let us carry with us the profound lessons we have learned from the mighty men. Their journeys of humility and teachability serve as timeless reminders of the transformative power of a humble heart. May we, like the mighty men, embrace the virtues of humility, seek wisdom, and cultivate a teachable spirit, for it is through these qualities that we, too, can rise to greatness and leave an indelible mark upon the world.

Within the chapters of their remarkable lives, the mighty men stand as testaments to the unwavering faith and unyielding trust they placed in the hands of the Almighty. As we embark on this extended journey, a new revelation emerges—Eliab, a valiant warrior whose faith and trust in God's providence added depth and significance to the narrative.

Eliab, with his steadfast devotion and unshakable belief, exemplified the unwavering faith that defined the mighty men. His presence in their midst brought a renewed sense of purpose and a profound understanding of the power of divine intervention. It was through his experiences that the mighty men witnessed firsthand the miraculous workings of God's providence in their lives.

Through the sacred scriptures and historical accounts, we unravel the lessons the mighty men gleaned about reliance on God's guidance. Their journeys, interwoven with moments of triumph and moments of trial, serve as living examples of the transformative power of prayer and the strength that flows from surrendering to God's will.

In the depths of their trials, the mighty men turned to prayer as their steadfast companion. With bended knees and hearts open to the heavens, they sought solace and strength in communion with the divine. Through prayer, they found clarity amidst confusion, courage amidst fear, and hope amidst despair.

The extended journey of exploration leads us to a remarkable encounter with Abigail, a woman of unwavering faith and profound wisdom. Abigail's presence brought a new dimension to the narrative, unveiling the transformative power of prayer in the lives of the mighty men. Her prayers, uttered with a blend of humility and conviction, became the catalyst for divine intervention and the turning of tides in the face of insurmountable odds.

As we delve deeper into their experiences, we witness the unwavering resolve and unwavering trust that anchored their souls. Their faith in God's presence and guidance became the bedrock upon which their actions were built. With every step they took, every decision they made, they entrusted their lives into the hands of the Divine, knowing that in His providence, they would find the strength and direction they needed.

Through the annals of history and the tapestry of their lives, we discover that reliance on God's guidance was not a mere concept but a tangible reality in the lives of the mighty men. It was their unwavering trust in God's providence that fortified their spirits, emboldened their actions, and enabled them to face the trials and tribulations that beset them.

Let us carry with us the profound lessons we have learned from the mighty men. Their unwavering faith and trust in God's providence serve as timeless reminders of the power that resides within us when we surrender ourselves to a higher purpose. May we, like the mighty men, anchor our souls in unwavering trust, knowing that in God's providence, we will find the strength to overcome any obstacle and the guidance to navigate life's tumultuous seas.

In the depths of their valorous journeys, a revelation emerges—a new figure, Josiah, whose unwavering dedication and unwavering loyalty adds a layer of depth to the narrative. It is within the tales of Josiah and his unwavering commitment to the brotherhood that we discover the true essence of the mighty men's unbreakable bond.

Josiah, a warrior with a heart ablaze for justice, joined the ranks of the mighty men, bringing with him a unique perspective and unwavering devotion. His introduction into the brotherhood breathed new life into their shared experiences, as his unwavering loyalty and steadfast spirit created an even stronger foundation for unity.

As we extend our exploration into this chapter, we unravel the lessons learned from the mighty men about the importance of unity, loyalty, and mutual support. Their journey, interwoven with tales of camaraderie forged on the battlefield, reveals the indomitable strength that emanates from standing shoulder to shoulder in the face of adversity.

The bond of brotherhood that coursed through the veins of the mighty men became the bedrock upon which their triumphs were built. Through thick and thin, they stood together, their unwavering loyalty like an unbreakable chain that linked their souls. Their unity was not just a means of survival but a testament to the power of solidarity and shared purpose.

In the heart of their shared experiences, we witness moments of celebration and moments of sorrow. Together, they weathered storms of uncertainty, bolstered by the unwavering support and encouragement of their brothers. Each victory was sweeter, each defeat easier to bear, because they faced them together.

It is through the tales of Josiah's unwavering commitment to the brotherhood that the true impact of their unbreakable bond becomes evident. His unwavering loyalty and steadfast spirit infused new energy into their shared experiences, reinforcing the importance of standing together as a united front.

As we reflect upon the lessons learned from the mighty men, their example resonates deeply within us. Their unbreakable bond of brotherhood reminds us of the strength that comes from unity, loyalty, and mutual support. It serves as a powerful reminder that we, too, can find solace, strength, and resilience in the embrace of those who stand beside us.

We carry with us the echoes of their stories—the echoes of camaraderie forged on the battlefield, the echoes of unwavering loyalty, and the echoes of the lasting impact of their brotherhood. May their example continue to inspire and guide us as we navigate our own journeys, reminding us that together, we are stronger, and that the bonds of brotherhood can withstand the tests of time.

In the vast tapestry of their remarkable tales, a new character emerges, Amos, a mighty man whose unwavering integrity and honorable demeanor add depth to the narrative. As we delve further into this chapter, we uncover the profound lessons woven into the fabric of the mighty men's lives—lessons that resonate with the importance of upholding moral principles, maintaining unwavering integrity, and acting with honor in every facet of life.

Amos, with his unyielding commitment to righteousness, joins the ranks of the mighty men, bringing with him a unique perspective and a steadfast adherence to moral values. His introduction into the brotherhood adds a vibrant hue to their collective journey, as his unwavering integrity becomes a shining example for all.

Within the vast expanse of their experiences, we witness moments where the mighty men are confronted with temptation—moments that test the strength of their character and integrity. Yet, time and again, they choose the path of righteousness, undeterred by the allure of compromise. Their resolute stance against moral compromises becomes a beacon, guiding readers towards the importance of upholding moral principles even in the face of adversity.

We unravel the stories of the mighty men and their encounters with moral dilemmas. Each tale serves as a testament to the unwavering commitment they held towards righteousness, acting as a moral compass that navigated them through the complexities of life. Their actions echo across time, inspiring readers to question their own choices and embrace the unwavering pursuit of integrity.

Amidst the ebb and flow of their collective journey, we witness the interplay of honor in every interaction. The mighty men's commitment to acting with honor in all aspects of life becomes a cornerstone of their character. They exemplify a code of conduct that transcends personal gain, choosing instead to prioritize integrity, respect, and fairness in their interactions with others.

It is through the stories of Amos and his unwavering commitment to righteousness that the significance of upholding moral principles becomes magnified. His steadfast dedication and honorable actions become a catalyst for deeper introspection, urging readers to reflect on their own moral compass and the choices they make in their daily lives.

The lessons resonating from the mighty men's unwavering integrity and honorable conduct linger within our hearts and minds. Their unwavering commitment to righteousness serves as a timeless lesson, reminding us of the enduring importance of upholding moral principles, maintaining our integrity in the face of temptation, and acting with honor in all aspects of life.

May their stories continue to inspire and guide us, reminding us of the profound impact that unwavering integrity and honorable actions can have in shaping not only our own lives but also the world around us.

In the midst of our contemplation, a new revelation emerges—a previously undiscovered account detailing the life of Benjamin, an unsung hero among the mighty men of David. As we delve deeper into this concluding chapter, we come to understand the profound impact Benjamin had on the legacy of these remarkable warriors, infusing the narrative with an added layer of inspiration and insight.

Reflecting upon the enduring legacy of the mighty men, we find ourselves captivated by the myriad of virtues they embodied. Loyalty, a cornerstone of their character, permeated every aspect of their lives. They remained steadfast in their allegiance to David, demonstrating unwavering support even in the face of adversity. Their unwavering loyalty was not simply an act of duty, but a testament to the depth of their character and the strength of their convictions.

Among the mighty men, there was one whose loyalty shone brilliantly, illuminating the path for others to follow. His name was Jonathan, a man whose unwavering devotion to David knew no bounds. From the moment they met, their souls intertwined in a bond of brotherhood that transcended mere friendship. Jonathan, the son of King Saul, recognized the anointing upon David and willingly relinquished his own claim to the throne, pledging his loyalty to David instead.

Their bond was forged through trials and tribulations, as they navigated the treacherous waters of political intrigue and the envy of others. Jonathan's loyalty was unwavering, even when it meant standing against his own father, who sought to harm David. In the face of adversity, Jonathan's unwavering support served as a beacon of hope and strength for David.

Alongside Jonathan, there stood Abigail, a woman of extraordinary wisdom and loyalty. Married to Nabal, a man of harsh and foolish disposition, Abigail possessed a discerning spirit and an unwavering commitment to righteousness. When Nabal provoked the wrath of David, Abigail intervened with grace and humility, sparing David from an act of vengeance and showing unwavering loyalty to both her husband and David.

The stories of Jonathan and Abigail, alongside the other mighty men, teach us the significance of standing by those we hold dear, regardless of the challenges that may arise. Their unwavering loyalty inspires us to examine our own relationships and commitments, urging us to remain steadfast and resolute even in the face of adversity.

In a world where loyalty can sometimes waver or be tested, the example of the mighty men reminds us of the enduring power of unwavering support. It challenges us to be people of integrity, consistently standing by those we love and remaining faithful to our commitments. Their stories teach us that loyalty is not a mere act of convenience, but a conscious choice to honor the bonds we have formed.

As we reflect upon the legacy of the mighty men, their unwavering loyalty becomes a call to action, urging us to cultivate and embody this virtue in our own lives. May their stories inspire us to stand by our friends, family, and loved ones, even in the face of adversity. May we learn from their example and become beacons of loyalty in a world that often seeks to tear us apart.

Courage, another virtue deeply embedded in the hearts of the mighty men, served as an unshakable foundation that propelled them to face seemingly insurmountable odds with unwavering determination. Their acts of valor and fearlessness on the battlefield became the stuff of legends, etching their names in the annals of history and inspiring generations to come. The stories of their courageous exploits stand as a testament to the incredible power of the human spirit and its ability to triumph over adversity.

One such exemplar of courage among the mighty men was Azariah, a warrior renowned for his unyielding bravery in the face of danger. Born into humble beginnings, Azariah had no noble lineage or grand reputation preceding him. However, what set him apart was his unwavering resolve to confront his fears head-on, regardless of the daunting challenges that lay before him.

In the midst of battle, when others would falter or retreat, Azariah stood firm, his heart filled with unwavering determination. With his weapon held high, he fearlessly charged into the fray, facing the enemy with unflinching resolve. The clash of swords and the cries of battle faded into the background as Azariah's courage blazed like an unquenchable fire within him.

Alongside Azariah stood another remarkable figure, Gideon, a man known for his unwavering courage and unwavering faith. Raised in the midst of adversity, Gideon's courage was forged in the crucible of trials and hardships. In the face of overwhelming odds, he led a small but resolute army against a formidable foe, trusting in the divine guidance and strength bestowed upon him.

Their acts of courage served as beacons of hope and inspiration, not only for their fellow warriors but for all who heard their tales. Through their example, the mighty men taught us that courage is not the absence of fear but the strength to persevere despite it. Their stories remind us that within each of us lies the potential for extraordinary bravery, waiting to be awakened and unleashed in the face of adversity.

As we walk through the battlefield of life, we can draw upon the courageous examples set by the mighty men to confront our own fears and rise above challenges. Their legacy encourages us to embrace our inner strength and face the unknown with unwavering determination. Through their stories, we find the courage to stand firm in the face of adversity, to press forward when others may retreat, and to inspire those around us to do the same.

The courage of the mighty men continues to resonate through the ages, reminding us that even in the darkest of times, courage can light the way. Their unwavering resolve to overcome obstacles serves as a guiding light, urging us to tap into our own reservoirs of bravery and forge ahead with determination. May their stories inspire us to be fearless in pursuit of our dreams, to stand tall in the face of adversity, and to write our own chapters of courage in the annals of history.

Humility, a virtue that radiated from the core of their being, shaped their interactions with others. Despite their remarkable achievements, the mighty men remained humble, recognizing that true greatness lies not in self-aggrandizement, but in service to others. Their humility becomes a guiding light, reminding us to approach life with a sense of modesty and genuine concern for the well-being of those around us.

Faith, a pillar upon which their lives were built, infused their every action with purpose and meaning. They possessed an unwavering trust in God's providence, seeking His guidance in every step they took. Their faith serves as a powerful reminder of the profound impact that a steadfast belief can have on our lives, instilling in us the courage to weather storms and the assurance that we are never alone.

Unity, forged through shared experiences and a common purpose, fortified their ranks. They stood shoulder to shoulder, bound by a sense of camaraderie that transcended individual aspirations. Together, they formed an unbreakable brotherhood, exemplifying the strength that comes from collective action. Their unity teaches us the value of collaboration, reminding us that by working together, we can achieve greatness beyond our wildest dreams.

Integrity, an unwavering commitment to moral principles, guided their every decision. They acted with honor, exemplifying the importance of honesty, fairness, and ethical conduct. Their unwavering adherence to a code of ethics becomes a guiding compass, urging us to embrace integrity in all aspects of our lives.

As we draw this chapter to a close, the stories of the mighty men resonate within us, reminding us that their virtues are not relics of a bygone era, but guiding principles that can shape our own lives. Inspired by their example, we are called to live lives of purpose, honor, and unwavering devotion to the causes we hold dear. The enduring legacy of the mighty men of David continues to inspire us, whispering to us that greatness is not an unattainable ideal, but a path we can walk when we embrace the virtues they embodied.

Don't miss out!

Visit the website below and you can sign up to receive emails whenever Casper Wamboko publishes a new book. There's no charge and no obligation.

https://books2read.com/r/B-A-TSHY-CWJLC

BOOKS 2 READ

Connecting independent readers to independent writers.

About the Author

Casper Wamboko is a professional writer who crafted his skills, doing blogs and social media articles. He is talented in writing articles on entertainment, technology and the environment.

Recently he decided to venture into the lucrative ebook market, with lots of projects in the works.

Read more at https://web.facebook.com/casper.wamboko.

About the Publisher

Delatech Solutions is an upcoming publishing house that has entered the market to support both traditional and indie based authors. It has the aim to also publish captivating stories that will keep the readers glued to their books. Welcome to Delatech Solutions Publications.